LAURIE JOY

Revolutionary Reads

Books to get you where you want to be, achieve your goals, break bad habits, get your customers to listen to you, get extraordinary results and change the world for the better

First edition

This book was professionally typeset on Reedsy.
Find out more at reedsy.com

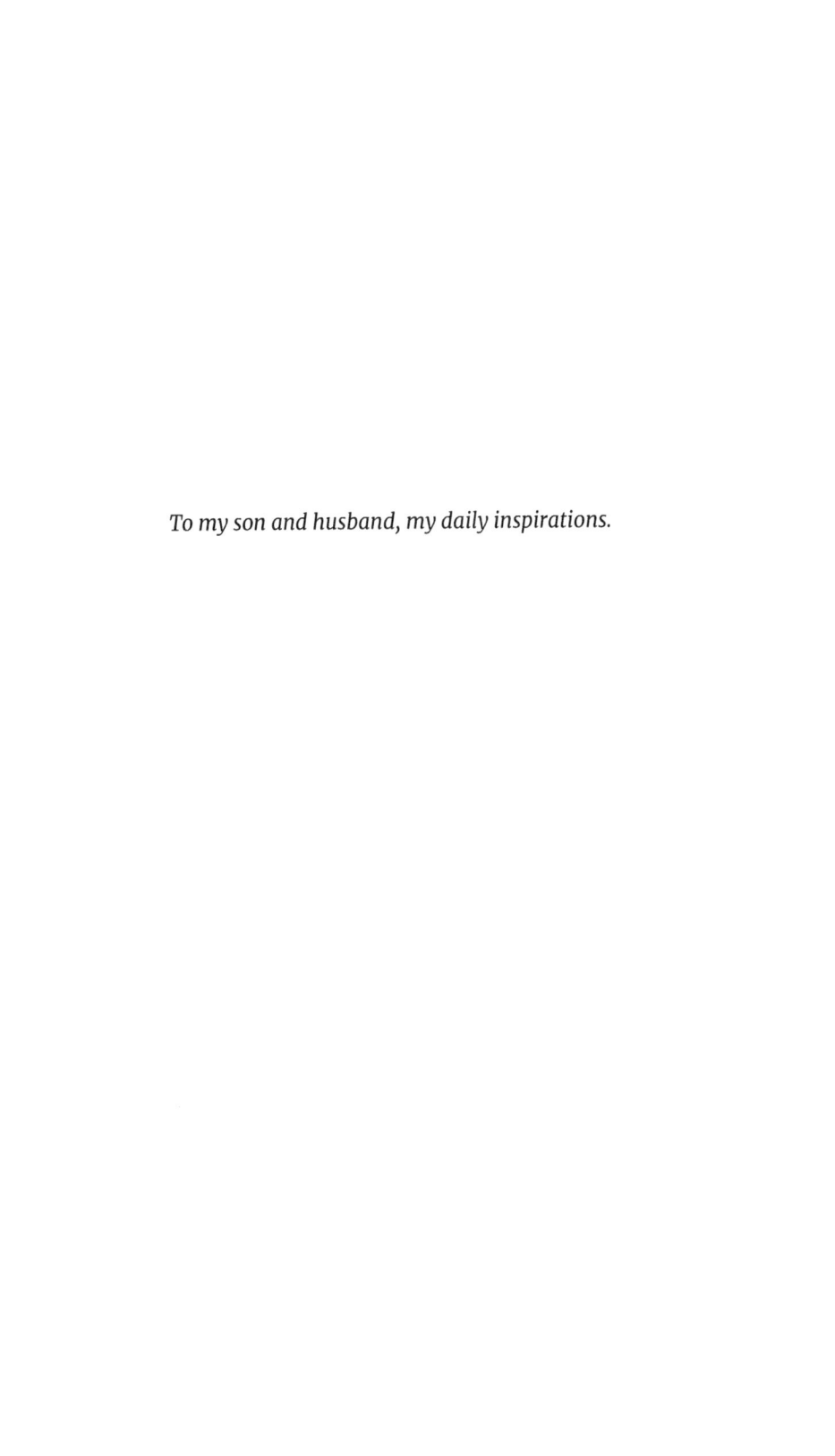

To my son and husband, my daily inspirations.

"Don't live the same year 75 times and call it a life."

Robin Sharma

Contents

1

Introduction

Welcome to a journey of self-discovery, empowerment, and transformation. In the bustling world of entrepreneurship, where dreams are nurtured and innovations thrive, "Revolutionary Reads" emerges as your guiding light—a carefully crafted selection of books that will not only propel you towards your goals but also reshape the very essence of your entrepreneurial spirit. Here, you'll find the keys to unlocking your potential, embracing intention, breaking free from old habits, and becoming an influential force in your industry.

In this series for entrepreneurs, you'll be introduced to the top five books that promise to change the trajectory of your professional and personal life. These books have been chosen with great care, each addressing important aspects of an entrepreneur's journey, from personal growth and mindset development to effective communication, productivity, and the power of good habits.

The carefully curated list includes:

- "The Success Principles" by Jack Canfield

- "Your Best Year Ever" by Michael Hyatt
- "Intentional Living" by John Maxwell
- "Atomic Habits" by James Clear
- "The One Thing" by Gary Keller

But before we delve into these life-changing books, let me share a bit of my own transformational journey. I have been a dedicated educator for over two decades, committed to the growth of my students within the four walls of a classroom. However, it was a serendipitous encounter with a health and wellness network marketing event that opened my eyes to a world beyond textbooks and lesson plans.

I attended an international event in support of a friend's remarkable transformation, and I found myself surrounded by 17,000 individuals who had chosen to rewrite their life stories. I witnessed ordinary people cross the stage, sharing their extraordinary journeys of personal and professional growth, all driven by their desire to make a positive impact in the world.

Sitting there amidst the electrifying energy of the crowd, I asked myself a profound question: "Why not me?" That weekend was a turning point in my life, igniting a fire within me to step out of my comfort zone and help others achieve their full potential.

Year after year, while I continued my role as an educator, I remained oblivious to the *revolutionary* transformations taking place in the entrepreneurial world. My professional development had exposed me to countless workshops and sessions, most of which fell short of meaningful change. It wasn't until that fateful weekend that I began my personal development journey in earnest.

They say that to grow a successful business, you must first grow yourself into a leader worth following. I embarked on this journey with an insatiable hunger for knowledge, starting with Jack Canfield's "The Success Principles." This book, with its relentless call to take 100% responsibility for my life, was the catalyst for profound change. It made me realize that I held the power to shape my destiny.

My copy of "The Success Principles" bears the scars of countless reads, its pages dog-eared and highlighted. It was the first step in my journey of self-discovery, one that led me to devour more and more personal development books with each passing day, month, and year.

Today, I feel compelled to share the transformative power of these books with you. They are written by some of the most exceptional minds who have not only inspired me but countless others on their entrepreneurial quests.

Entrepreneurship is an arduous path, demanding a ton of dedication and persistence. It is a journey of self-discovery, perseverance, and the relentless pursuit of excellence. Yet, it is a journey that holds immeasurable rewards (if you're an entrepreneur, you know this)!

This book is your gateway to the magic hidden within the pages of the top five books I've carefully selected for you. Inside, you'll find a brief summary, the three chapters that resonated most with me, powerful quotes that will leave you in awe, and insights that will expand your thinking.

Life is too short not to be an entrepreneur, and it's equally too short to waste on subpar literature. As we explore these books together, remember that you're not alone in your entrepreneurial pursuit. This book is here to guide you, inspire you, and help you tap into the boundless potential that resides within.

So, here's to you—the entrepreneur who dances to the beat of their own drum, who has sacrificed, persevered, and pursued greatness. Thank you for choosing this book, for being a part of my dreams, and for allowing me to contribute to the dream of building a library for children in Kenya through the charity, Village Impact, founded by the remarkable Stu and Amy McLaren. A portion of the proceeds from this book will go to funding that library.

As we venture forward, I invite you to connect with me on social media, @lauriejoy.biz and share your support for the library,

I hope you savour every word of this book, and more importantly, I hope it leads you to other life-altering reads. Cheers to your ultimate success and to the library we dream of building together!

With that being said, let's jump right in!

Laurie Joy

2

A Summary of Success Principles by Jack Canfield

Hey there, you unstoppable success seekers! Let's dive into "Success Principles" by Jack Canfield, your golden ticket to a life that's off-the-charts amazing. This isn't your run-of-the-mill book; it's your roadmap to unlocking your boundless potential and turning your wildest dreams into your everyday reality. Get ready for a life-changing journey that'll have you screaming, "I've got this!"

So, what's the lowdown on this book? It's like having a personal success sage in your back pocket. Jack Canfield, the mastermind of personal growth, drops a whopping 64 game-changing principles right in your lap. This isn't just any book; it's a treasure trove of wisdom, a field guide to living your most epic life.

But here's where it gets juicy: Success isn't just about doing things differently; it's about becoming someone different. Canfield's book isn't just a self-help guide; it's your invitation to transform into the most extraordinary version of yourself.

Now, what's the one mind-blowing takeaway that will rock your world? Brace yourself for this gem: You're not a passenger in the grand voyage of your life; you're the captain of your own ship. This book isn't just a manual; it's your rallying call to step up, take charge, and steer your life with unshakable confidence.

And how does this book deliver the goods? It's a game-changer of cosmic proportions. You'll gain the clarity to set goals so colossal they'll make your heart race. Challenges will morph into opportunities, and setbacks will become your launch pads to epic comebacks. Your journey will shift from a foggy labyrinth of uncertainty to a thrilling adventure with you firmly at the wheel.

But hold onto your hats, because here come the practical nuggets of wisdom Canfield serves up: from setting goals that are so clear they practically scream at you, to taking action so massive it'll send shockwaves through your universe. From rewiring your mindset for success to putting your fears in their place, Canfield leaves no stone unturned.

He'll dismantle your self-doubt, kick scarcity thinking to the curb, and install an abundance mindset that'll have you dancing through life. You'll learn to embrace challenges, leverage setbacks, and turn your wildest dreams into everyday reality.

Whether you're hell-bent on amassing wealth, nurturing relationships, or chasing your passions with unbridled fervour, Canfield's principles will be your secret sauce to success (say that five times fast)!

So, my fellow dream weavers and goal crushers, here's your playbook for conquering the universe. "Success Principles" by Jack Canfield is your North Star, your treasure map, and your rocket fuel. It's time to flip the script on mediocrity, unleash your inner superhero, and create a life that'll make you shout, "Is this even real?!"

If you're itching to embark on a journey that'll make you the hero of your own story and rocket your success into the stratosphere, then grab this book. Say sayonara to average, and get ready to unleash the extraordinary life you were born to live.

3

The Essential Trio: Must-Read Chapters: Success Principles

1.Taking 100% Responsibility for Your Life

Calling all entrepreneurs, let's talk about taking charge of your destiny, shall we? This chapter is the holy grail of success because it's all about owning your life, lock, stock, and barrel. Canfield throws down the gauntlet and says, "Hey, if you want to make it big, you've got to take 100% responsibility for your life." That means no more blame games, no more excuses. It's about embracing your power to steer the ship of your life, no matter the storms you encounter. For entrepreneurs, this is the secret sauce because it empowers you to transform challenges into opportunities, make decisions with conviction, and lead your business to glory. So, are you ready to be the fearless captain of your entrepreneurial journey? I sure hope so because this chapter is your ticket to rule the world.

2. Believe in Yourself

Entrepreneurs, gather 'round, because we're diving deep into the magical land of self-belief. Canfield knows that entrepreneurship can sometimes feel like a wild, unpredictable ride. But guess what? Believing in yourself is your secret weapon. This chapter is all about turning self-doubt into unwavering self-confidence. It's about strutting your stuff, embracing your brilliance, and telling that inner critic to take a hike. When you believe in yourself, you become a force to be reckoned with. You make bold decisions, inspire others, and turn your entrepreneurial dreams into reality. So, stand tall, entrepreneurs, because you've got the power within you to conquer any business mountain. This chapter is your call to arms, your reminder to say, "I am unstoppable!"

3. Create Successful Relationships

Ah, relationships – the heart and soul of entrepreneurship. This chapter is your guide to becoming a relationship rockstar. Canfield spills the beans on effective communication, empathy, and the art of building connections that last. For entrepreneurs, this is pure gold. Building fruitful relationships isn't just about schmoozing; it's about creating a tribe that supports your mission. It's about negotiation wizardry, networking finesse, and winning over hearts and minds. Successful entrepreneurs know that relationships are their secret weapon. So, dive into this chapter with gusto, and master the art of creating bonds that'll take your business to the stratosphere. After all, in the world of entrepreneurship, relationships are your rocket fuel.

4

Quotable Quotations: Success Principles

1. "Don't worry about failures, worry about the chances you miss when you don't even try."

Oh, sweet entrepreneurs, let this gem marinate in your mind for a minute. Canfield's telling you that failure is not the enemy – missed opportunities are. How many times have you held back because you feared falling flat on your face? This quote screams at you: "Go big or go home!" It's an invitation to kick fear in the teeth and take those leaps of faith. Because every time you try, you're one step closer to success. Remember, those who dare to fail greatly are the ones who change the world.

2. "Everything you want is on the other side of fear."

Entrepreneurs, this one's a game-changer. Canfield's dropping truth bombs left and right. Your wildest dreams, the big vision you have for your business – they're all waiting for you, just beyond that intimidating wall called fear. So, what are you going to do? You're going to punch fear in the face and charge ahead like the fearless trailblazer you are. Success, abundance, and all your heart's desires are on the other side. Take a deep breath, embrace your courage, and let's go conquer the world together!

3. "You are not given a dream unless you have the capacity to fulfill it."

Let this quote from Canfield sink in deep. It's a cosmic reminder that your dreams weren't randomly assigned; they're tailor-made for you. That audacious vision you have for your business? It's not a pipe dream; it's your destiny. This quote is a kick in the pants, telling you to stop doubting yourself. You've got the skills, the grit, and the heart to turn that dream into reality. It's not a matter of "if"; it's a matter of "when." So, get out there, own your greatness, and make that dream your glorious truth.

5

Actionable Insights: Success Principles

Alright, my entrepreneurial warriors, listen up because I'm about to drop the mother of all takeaways from "Success Principles" by Jack Canfield, and it's going to rock your world. This book is here to teach you that you are the master of your fate, the captain of your ship, and the CEO of your life.

What this means for you, dear entrepreneur, is that you're not just running a business; you're crafting your destiny. It's not about merely reacting to the tides of life – it's about creating a tidal wave of success that sweeps you to greatness. The difference this book will make is colossal. It's going to transform you from someone who merely dreams about success to someone who lives and breathes it.

Picture this: you wake up every day, not just ready to face the entrepreneurial battlefield, but excited to conquer it. Your mindset shifts from "I hope this works" to "I've got this, and nothing can stop me." Your business isn't just a venture; it's a mission, a manifestation of your deepest desires, and it thrives under your unwavering belief.

Your outlook on life? It's as vibrant as a double rainbow after a storm. You see challenges as opportunities, setbacks as setups for epic comebacks, and failures as stepping stones to success. Your confidence soars, and that "imposter syndrome" you once battled? It's history.

But here's the kicker: the book isn't just about making you a business superstar; it's about making you an all-around badass. You'll take these principles into your personal life, your relationships, your health – and you'll be unstoppable there too.

So, fellow entrepreneurs, when you dive into "Success Principles," brace yourself for a seismic shift. You'll no longer be a spectator of your own life; you'll be the star of your own show. Get ready to unleash the force within, claim your dreams, and say, "Success, I'm coming for you!"

6

Unpacking Your Best Year Ever by Michael Hyatt

Alright, all you go-getters and dream-chasers, prepare for a life-altering journey through the pages of "Your Best Year Ever" by the exceptional Michael Hyatt. This book isn't just a guide; it's your ticket to transform your life and your entrepreneurial journey. Hyatt takes you by the hand and leads you through the art of setting and achieving goals like a true visionary.

He begins by emphasizing the importance of clear, compelling goals. These aren't just wishes jotted down on a piece of paper; they're the driving force that propels you forward, igniting your passion and unearthing your untapped potential. Hyatt understands that without a well-defined target, you're navigating a stormy sea without a compass. Ar, matey!

But hold onto your seats because he doesn't stop there. Hyatt unveils a systematic approach that breaks down your grand aspirations into manageable, actionable steps. No longer will you be overwhelmed by the enormity of your dreams. You'll have a roadmap, a series of checkpoints, and the unwavering confidence to make your dreams a reality. Now who doesn't want that?

Now, let's talk about those pesky obstacles. Hyatt knows that life is not all sunshine and rainbows, especially in the entrepreneurial world. He equips you with the tools to overcome any roadblocks that stand in your way. He guides you to identify your limiting beliefs and blast through them with the force of a thousand entrepreneurial dynamos.

And here's the kicker – it's not just about achieving your goals; it's about becoming the person you need to be to achieve them. Hyatt's wisdom goes beyond material success; it's about personal growth, resilience, and unshakeable confidence.

In "Your Best Year Ever," Hyatt introduces you to the concept of the "LifeScore Assessment." This invaluable tool assesses ten core areas of your life, giving you a crystal-clear snapshot of where you currently stand. It's a reality check, but it's also a revelation. Once you see the gaps between where you are and where you want to be, you'll be itching to fill them in.

But what truly sets this book apart is Hyatt's infectious optimism. He doesn't just provide you with a roadmap; he becomes your cheerleader, your mentor, and your partner in success. His words are a constant reminder that you are capable of more than you think, and every obstacle is a mere stepping stone on your path to greatness.

In a world filled with uncertainty, "Your Best Year Ever" becomes your North Star, guiding you through the tumultuous entrepreneurial waters with unwavering certainty. This book isn't just about making this year great; it's about making every year from now on your best year ever.

So, entrepreneurs, if you're ready to turn your aspirations into reality, if you're prepared to set audacious goals and chase them relentlessly, and if you're willing to embrace personal growth like never before, then grab a copy of "Your Best Year Ever." Your journey to success begins on the very first page, and the results will be nothing short of extraordinary.

7

The Essential Trio: Must-Read Chapters: Your Best Year Ever

1.How to Harness the Power of a Big Why

Strap in, fellow entrepreneurs, because this chapter is your ticket to goal-setting glory! Michael Hyatt is about to drop some truth bombs that will blow your mind and send your ambitions soaring. Why is it a must-read? Because it's all about your "why" – that magical, soul-stirring reason that gets you out of bed in the morning. You see, your "why" isn't just a goal; it's an emotional powerhouse that propels you through challenges and setbacks. Hyatt's wisdom will teach you how to unearth that golden "why" and make it the rocket fuel for your dreams. Get ready to set goals with heart and rocket toward success like the badass entrepreneur you are!

2. The Not-So-Secret Secret of Productive Achievers

Productivity, my entrepreneurial warriors, is the name of the game, and this chapter is your treasure map to the land of ultimate efficiency. Michael Hyatt isn't here to spill some ordinary productivity tips; he's here to reveal the not-so-secret secret. It's all about creating "margin" in your life – that heavenly space between your tasks and your limits. In this chapter, you'll learn how to reclaim your time, become a productivity powerhouse, and slay your entrepreneurial goals with ease. Say goodbye to overwhelm and hello to a life where productivity is your middle name. Get ready to conquer your to-do list like the productivity maven you were born to be!

3. What to Do When You Get Stuck

Buckle up, my resilient comrades in entrepreneurship, because this chapter is your lifeline when the entrepreneurial roller coaster throws you for a loop. Michael Hyatt understands that every entrepreneur faces moments of being stuck, stalled, or downright discouraged. In this chapter, he equips you with battle-tested strategies to blast through obstacles and stay on course. It's all about resilience, my friends – that unwavering determination to persevere when the going gets tough. Hyatt's wisdom will teach you how to navigate the inevitable bumps in the road and come out on the other side stronger than ever. Get ready to conquer every setback like the fearless entrepreneur you were born to be!

8

Quotable Quotations: Your Best Year Ever

1. "The future is not a result of choices among alternative paths offered by the present but a place that is created—created first in the mind and will, created next in activity. The future is not some place we are going to, but one we are creating."

Picture this, you unstoppable entrepreneur! This quote is your personal reminder that your future isn't some distant, far-off land you hope to reach someday. No, it's a blank canvas waiting for your bold strokes of genius. Your choices today are the paintbrushes you wield to craft the masterpiece of tomorrow. As an entrepreneur, you're not a passenger on this journey; you're the captain charting uncharted waters. Get ready to embrace the power you hold to create the epic future you've always imagined!

2. "Instead of letting your hardships and failures discourage or exhaust you, let them inspire you."

Listen up, fearless trailblazer! This quote flips the script on adversity. It's a rallying cry for every entrepreneur who's tasted the bitter tang of setbacks. Instead of letting those tough times bring you down, let them light a fire within. Your hardships and failures are like rocket fuel for your entrepreneurial spirit. They're the challenges that dare you to rise, the puzzles that beg you to solve them, and the stepping stones that elevate you to greatness. Embrace them as the fiery crucible in which your entrepreneurial metal is forged.

3. "Your ability to achieve your goals will be largely determined by your ability to focus, persist, and endure, regardless of what life throws at you."

This quote hammers home a fundamental truth – your success isn't a lottery; it's the result of your unwavering focus, willful persistence, and unbreakable endurance. In a world teeming with distractions and unexpected challenges, your ability to stay locked on your goals, persevere through the darkest hours, and stand tall when life throws its curveballs is your secret weapon. You're not just chasing dreams; you're charging headfirst into them with relentless determination. These quotes are your anthem of your journey, reminding you that your future is a canvas, your setbacks are stepping stones, and your success is forged by your fierce focus, persistence, and endurance. Get ready to conquer your entrepreneurial world like the unstoppable force you were born to be!

9

Actionable Insights: Your Best Year Ever

Michael Hyatt is about to blow the lid off your limitations and redefine your entire hustle. Ready for the takeaway that'll light your entrepreneurial spirit on fire? Your past? Irrelevant. Your future? A canvas you get to paint.

So, how does this revolutionize your entrepreneurial game? This isn't just about setting goals; it's a cosmic invitation to design a future that's your own masterpiece. We're not talking about vanilla goals; we're talking about SMARTER goals – Specific, Measurable, Achievable, Relevant, Time-bound, and Energizing. Oh, and let's leave room for surprises because, let's face it, life's a wild ride.

But wait, there's more. Hyatt's dropping wisdom bombs on creating space for the magic to happen. Margin is your secret weapon against the chaos. It's not about doing more; it's about doing more with intention, preventing burnout, and making room for your creative genius to shine.

Imagine this: deadlines aren't stress bombs; they're your secret sauce for turning dreams into concrete, deadline-driven goals. Hyatt's your partner in crime, transforming wishful thinking into tangible, kick-ass goals. Your dreams just got a roadmap!

And here's the mic-drop moment: the real goal isn't the destination; it's the incredible version of yourself you become on the journey. It's not just about crossing off achievements; it's a full-blown metamorphosis.

So, what's the one main difference? Those armed with "Your Best Year Ever" aren't just achieving success; they're orchestrating a symphony of victories across every damn area of life. Your business isn't on an island; it's part of a life that's a relentless pursuit of extraordinary. Ready to turn wishes into a reality that's as awesome as you are? Let's make this year YOURS, unapologetically and unforgettable.

10

Insights from Atomic Habits by James Clear

Alright, my fellow entrepreneurs, buckle up because I've got a treasure trove of wisdom for you in "Atomic Habits" by James Clear. This book isn't just a game-changer; it's your ticket to a life and business on steroids. Clear's masterpiece is all about the tiny, almost invisible habits that can launch you into the stratosphere of success.

Picture this: you're not merely dreaming of epic achievements; you're taking small, consistent actions every day to reach your goals. That's the beauty of "Atomic Habits" - it's all about making big waves with tiny ripples.

Clear takes you on a journey deep into the heart of habit formation. He unveils the secret sauce of habit transformation - the habit loop. This loop consists of four key components: cue, craving, response, and reward. Understanding this loop is like peeking behind the curtain of your own mind. It's where habits are born, and it's where your potential for greatness lies.

But James doesn't just leave you with the theory. He serves up the science and practical strategies, giving you the tools to rewire your brain for success. Consider it a masterclass in the psychology of habit formation, a golden ticket to entrepreneurial neuro-hacking.

Now, here's the goldmine: those tiny, seemingly insignificant atomic habits. They're your secret sauce to lasting success. Think about the snowball effect of daily, minuscule improvements in your productivity, networking skills, customer relationships, or any facet of your entrepreneurial journey. That's the atomic power in action.

But it gets better. "Atomic Habits" introduces the concept of identity-based habits. It's not just about what you do; it's about who you become. By aligning your identity with your goals, habits become second nature because they're an integral part of your new, improved self.

Imagine this in your entrepreneurial voyage: no more chasing fleeting bursts of motivation. Instead, you're crafting systems and habits that naturally sync with your goals, day in and day out. You're not just "doing" things; you're "becoming" the entrepreneur you aspire to be.

But how do you turn this newfound wisdom into concrete action? Clear's got your back with a straightforward framework for habit creation: make it obvious, make it attractive, make it easy, and make it satisfying. This is your entrepreneur's toolkit for crafting habits that stick, whether it's optimizing your workspace, nailing your pitch, or streamlining your business operations.

In the entrepreneurial cosmos, "Atomic Habits" isn't just a book; it's your secret weapon. By embracing the power of small, consistent actions, you'll unlock the full scope of your entrepreneurial prowess. No more battling procrastination or inconsistency. It's time to embody the high-performing entrepreneur within.

So, fellow entrepreneurs, grasp the might of atomic habits, zero in on those small but potent actions, and witness your entrepreneurial odyssey undergo a magnificent transformation. Success isn't about wishful thinking; it's about taking precise, atomic steps daily. Don't just read this book; live it. Your entrepreneurial destiny beckons, and it's time to respond with atomic precision.

11

The Essential Trio: Must-Read Chapters: Atomic Habits

1.How Your Habits Shape Your Identity (and Vice Versa)

Picture this, my entrepreneurial comrades: your habits aren't just little routines you do daily. Oh no, they're the architects of your identity. They mold you, shape you, and define you. Clear's chapter takes you on a journey inside your own mind. It's where you'll discover that you're not just a product of your habits; your habits are a product of who you believe you are. For you, my savvy entrepreneurs, this means recognizing that you're not just running a business; you're BECOMING a business wizard. So, dive into this chapter and learn how to redefine your identity as a high-achieving entrepreneur. Watch how your habits transform to align with your extraordinary vision.

2.How to Build Better Habits in 4 Simple Steps

Now, let's talk about action, my fellow go-getters. Clear's four-step habit-building framework is like having a treasure map to success. It all starts with a cue, igniting that craving, following through with the response, and topping it off with a sweet reward. Entrepreneurs, this is your roadmap to creating and nurturing habits that can turbocharge your business endeavours. Think about it: craving the thrill of productivity, responding with laser-focused work, and rewarding yourself with milestones achieved. It's a habit loop that transforms you into the entrepreneur of your dreams. This chapter is your blueprint for building habits that'll catapult your entrepreneurial journey into the stratosphere.

3.How to Design Your Environment for Success

Imagine your surroundings as the stage for your entrepreneurial success story. In this chapter, Clear reveals the magical connection between your environment and your habits. Entrepreneurs, it's time to take control of your stage. Design an environment that doesn't just support your dreams but propels them. Your workspace becomes a launchpad for innovation, collaboration, and productivity. It's not just about arranging furniture; it's about creating a culture of success within your business ecosystem. Dive into this chapter, my entrepreneurial trailblazers, and learn how to craft an environment that nurtures your entrepreneurial spirit, ignites your creativity, and fuels your journey to the top.

12

Quotable Quotations: Atomic Habits

1. "You do not rise to the level of your goals. You fall to the level of your systems."

Yes, it's worth repeating. Tattoo it on your entrepreneur soul. Goals are splendid, but systems are your secret weapon. Your habits are the threads weaving the tapestry of your success. Embrace this truth, and watch your entrepreneurial journey soar.

2. "You should be far more concerned with your current trajectory than with your current results."

Feel the mic drop? Your results today are mere echoes of your past habits. But, darling entrepreneur, focus on the trajectory. Are your habits propelling you toward greatness? It's not just about the now; it's about the phenomenal future you're crafting.

3. "You don't have to be the victim of your environment. You can also be the architect of it."

Alright, entrepreneurs, listen up as James Clear drops the truth bomb: 'You don't have to be the victim of your environment. You can also be the architect of it.' Forget playing the victim; it's time to channel your inner architect. Picture yourself not just navigating your surroundings but actively crafting them to fuel your journey to triumph. You're not at the mercy of your environment; you're the powerhouse designing it. So, grab your creative tools, shape a space that ignites your brilliance, and strut into the arena of success you're crafting. Your environment, your rules—because, darling, you're the amazing architect of your destiny.

13

Actionable Insights: Atomic Habits

When you crack open "Atomic Habits" by James Clear, there's one colossal takeaway that's about to rock your entrepreneurial world: Your habits? They're not just those daily routines; they're the architects of your destiny! This revelation? It's not just a lightbulb moment; it's a supernova of transformation, and it's going to change the game for you.

Picture this: Your habits are the secret sauce that'll turn your business from a so-so venture into a powerhouse of success. No more floundering or inconsistency. This book is your secret weapon, and it's going to empower you to turn your daily grind into a well-oiled machine of prosperity.

But that's just the tip of the iceberg! Reading "Atomic Habits" is like a mindset makeover on steroids. Say goodbye to self-doubt and playing small. You're going to step into the shoes of the entrepreneurial legend you've always dreamed of becoming. Your mindset? It's going to shift gears from 'I can't' to 'heck yeah, I can!' It's all about envisioning those big, audacious goals and taking the world by storm.

And guess what? Your workspace? It's not just a desk and some chairs; it's your fortress of innovation, your sanctuary of creativity, your playground of success. This book? It's your ticket to designing an environment that screams 'let's do this!' Imagine a place where your ideas flow like a river, and your team's energy is off the charts. That's what's waiting for you.

So, bottom line? Reading "Atomic Habits" is like unleashing your inner superhero. You'll be the star, the director, and the driving force behind your success story. It's not just about building habits; it's about becoming the unstoppable, world-changing entrepreneur you were born to be.

Grab that book, my fellow business ninja, and let it ignite the atomic spark within. Get ready to embrace the art of habit formation like the superhero you are. Your journey starts now, and trust me, the difference it's going to make? It's nothing short of mind-blowing. You've got this!

14

Key Lessons from Building a StoryBrand by Donald Miller

P icture this: You're in a bustling marketplace, surrounded by vendors shouting their offers, each trying to grab your attention. Amidst the chaos, there's one merchant who doesn't shout louder but tells a compelling story that captivates you. That's what "How to Build A Storybrand" by Donald Miller teaches you to be - the storyteller who stands out in the noisy world of business.

Miller's book is your backstage pass to the magic of storytelling, a superpower that can transform your brand and business. He's your guide on a journey to create a brand message so crystal clear, it slices through the clutter like a laser beam through fog.

At its core, this book is all about turning your brand message into an irresistible story. Miller doesn't just talk about the theory; he gives you a roadmap, an ancient treasure map for the modern entrepreneur. He reveals that the secret sauce is in clarifying your message.

So, why do some brands thrive while others sink into oblivion? It's all about clarity. Miller unravels this mystery by introducing the hero's journey, a storytelling framework as old as time. In this narrative, your customer is the hero, facing challenges, and your brand? Well, it's the Yoda guiding them through their epic quest.

Miller peels back the layers of this framework, illustrating how it plays out in the real business world. He urges you to let go of the hero cape and embrace the guide role. Your customer deserves the spotlight. They're the hero; you're the mentor showing them the path to victory.

But what good is a message if it's buried under jargon and confusion? Miller introduces "The Grunt Test," a genius way to check if your message makes sense. If it doesn't pass this test, you're back to the drawing board. But don't worry; Miller provides practical strategies to craft a message that not only passes but excels.

As you devour the pages, you'll discover the magic of empathy, clarity, and simplicity in storytelling. Miller shares real-world examples and case studies, revealing how giants like Apple and Disney have mastered these principles.

15

The Essential Trio: Must-Read Chapters: Building a StoryBrand

1.A Character:

Alright, you incredible entrepreneurs, let's kick things off with a bang! In this mind-blowing chapter, Donald Miller invites you to embrace the idea that your brand is not just a logo—it's a freakin' character in an epic story. Get ready to infuse personality into your business because, honey, it's time to make your brand memorable, relatable, and downright irresistible. This isn't about selling a product; it's about starring in a narrative where your brand is the hero everyone cheers for.

2. And Meets a Guide:

Picture this: You're not just a business; you're the wise sage guiding your customers through the tumultuous journey of their problems. In this marvelous chapter, Miller shows you how to be the Yoda to your customers' Luke Skywalker. It's not about pushing a product; it's about becoming the trusted guide your customers can't imagine navigating this crazy world without. Get ready to be the beacon of wisdom your customers have been desperately searching for.

3. The Simple SB7 Framework:

Get ready to strap on your branding boots because in the "Simple SB7 Framework," Donald Miller is about to take your brand from zero to hero! This chapter is your backstage pass to crafting a brand that isn't just a logo; it's a freakin' character with personality and pizzazz. Dive into real problems, become the ultimate guide, and unleash a plan that has your customers screaming, "I want in!" Your call-to-action won't just be heard; it'll be felt in the hearts of your audience. No more tiptoeing around failure; position your brand as the superhero saving the day. And let's not forget the grand finale – success. This isn't just a purchase; it's a journey that leaves your customers cheering for an encore. With the SB7 Framework, your brand is not just a brand; it's a storytelling sensation that commands the stage.

16

Quotable Quotations: Building a StoryBrand

1."The customer is the hero, not your brand."

Darling, in this blockbuster of business, your customer deserves the starring role. Your brand? It's the director, the visionary behind the scenes, making sure your customer's journey is nothing short of Oscar-worthy. Let their story shine, and watch your brand become the box office hit.

2."If you confuse, you'll lose."

Let's talk clarity because nothing kills the entrepreneurial vibe faster than a plot twist of confusion. In a world drowning in noise, simplicity is your entrepreneurial crown jewel. Lose the confusion, and let your brand stand tall in the spotlight of crystal-clear brilliance. It's not just a mantra; it's a runway-ready strategy."

3."The goal of a brand is to become a verb."

Your brand not just as a noun but a freaking verb! It's not just a name;

it's an action, a movement. Becoming the verb in your customer's life is the holy grail of branding. Be the 'google' of your industry, and let your brand legacy be etched in the dictionary of success.

17

Actionable Insights: Building a StoryBrand

Alright, fellow trailblazers, after soaking up the brilliance of "How to Build A Storybrand" by Donald Miller, here's the golden nugget: your brand isn't just a business; it's a character in a blockbuster story.

The difference this revelation makes is colossal—it transforms your approach to branding from mundane to magnificent. As an entrepreneur, you'll no longer just sell products; you'll craft an irresistible narrative that captivates your audience. Your business becomes the guide, the hero, and the trusted advisor in the epic story of your customers' lives. Get ready for a mindset shift that transcends the ordinary; your brand is about to steal the spotlight, leaving a legacy that echoes in the hearts of your audience. It's not just about selling; it's about storytelling, and that, my friends, is the game-changer for hard working entrepreneurs ready to make waves.

18

Insights from The One Thing by Gary Keller

I n the realm of entrepreneurial self-improvement, "The One Thing" by Gary Keller is like the holy grail of focus and achievement. This book takes you on an exhilarating ride, teaching you the art of honing in on the most pivotal aspects of your life and business. Instead of frantically juggling a dozen tasks, you're zeroing in on that one magnificent, game-changing thing that will propel you forward faster than you ever imagined.

Keller's message is pure and potent − stop spreading yourself too thin and start concentrating your energy on what truly matters. He unleashes the magic of the "domino effect" before your eyes, demonstrating how one significant achievement can set off a domino chain reaction of success in all areas of your life. This book doesn't just throw concepts at you; it arms you with actionable strategies to put the "one thing" philosophy into immediate practice.

In "The One Thing," you'll encounter inspiring stories and real-life examples that showcase the astonishing results of unwavering focus. Keller's "focusing question" is your secret weapon. Whenever you're faced with a choice, it whispers in your ear, asking, *"What's the one thing I can do, such that by doing it, everything else will be easier or unnecessary?"* It's your compass, guiding you toward your North Star – your most crucial task.

The book hammers home the idea that success isn't about doing everything right; it's about doing the right thing at the right time. Say goodbye to distractions and multitasking; Keller shows you the path to productivity nirvana. By tuning out the noise and devoting yourself to your "one thing," you'll emerge as a productivity powerhouse.

This book will leave you with an unshakable belief in the power of focus and prioritization. You'll ditch overwhelm, make better decisions, and unleash your full potential. The core lesson? If you want exceptional results, you've got to pinpoint your top priority and channel your energy there.

In the end, "The One Thing" gives entrepreneurs a treasure map to remarkable success. It's all about identifying your numero uno, eliminating the distractions, and embracing the beauty of unwavering focus. Gary Keller is your sherpa on this transformative journey, promising to turn your entrepreneurial adventure into a symphony of singular success.

19

The Essential Trio: Must-Read Chapters: The One Thing

1.The ONE Thing

Embrace the magic of "The ONE Thing" and unlock your true potential. In this chapter, you'll discover the transformative power of pinpointing your most critical task – your "one thing." It's not about doing everything but about doing the right thing. As an entrepreneur, this chapter is your ticket to laser-like focus, increased productivity, and achieving remarkable results. Get ready to kick overwhelm to the curb and take charge of your destiny!

2.Multitasking

Say goodbye to the myth of multitasking and hello to supercharged productivity. In this eye-opening chapter, Gary Keller reveals why juggling multiple tasks at once is a recipe for disaster. Entrepreneurs, it's time to stop spreading yourself thin and start concentrating your energy on your "one thing." By understanding the perils of multitasking, you'll gain the clarity and freedom to channel your efforts where they matter most.

3.The Focusing Question

Get ready to ignite your success with the game-changing Focusing Question. This chapter introduces you to a simple yet profound query that can revolutionize your decision-making process. As an entrepreneur, you'll learn how to cut through the noise and identify your most impactful actions. The Focusing Question becomes your compass, guiding you toward your "one thing" and ensuring your daily efforts align with your long-term goals. Get ready to supercharge your journey with this powerful tool!

20

Quotable Quotations: The One Thing

1."Success is about doing the right thing, not about doing everything right."

Success isn't a meticulous checklist; it's a wild dance. It's about sashaying towards the right thing, not drowning in an exhaustive to-do list. So, my friend, twirl towards success with the grace of focused action.

2."You need to be doing fewer things for more effect instead of doing more things with side effects."

It's not about being a jack-of-all-trades; it's about being a maestro (Fresh Wes) of impact. Focus your energy where it matters, and watch the symphony of success play out with a resounding melody of brilliance.

3."The key to success is figuring out the one thing you can do, such that by doing it, everything else will be easier or unnecessary."

Unlock success by finding that one thing that lights your soul on fire. It's not just a key; it's a magical wand making everything else bow to your entrepreneurial prowess.

21

Actionable Insights: The One Thing

Alright, fellow trailblazer, brace yourself for the golden nugget—the one thing that'll have you high-fiving the universe. The big takeaway? It's time to ditch the overwhelm and embrace the power of focus. This book is your backstage pass to a game-changing mindset shift.

Picture this: clarity so sharp it cuts through the noise, decisions so on point and a business game so strong it practically runs itself.

The magic here is all about honing in on 'The One Thing.' It's the secret sauce to rocking your entrepreneur journey. Imagine waking up every day with a clear target, knowing exactly where to direct your energy for maximum impact. No more spinning wheels, no more drowning in the sea of tasks—just pure, unadulterated badassery.

This book isn't just a read; it's your roadmap to sanity and success. It'll recalibrate your approach, redefine your priorities, and have you strutting through your business with the swagger of a conquering hero. Get ready to be the entrepreneur who not only survives but thrives. It's time to kick ass, take names, and make 'The One Thing' your superpower. Let's do this!

22

Conclusion

A nd there we have it. I hope you enjoyed a little snippet of those books and what they shared as much as I enjoyed writing it. I invite you to reflect on the incredible journey we've embarked upon together. Through the pages of these extraordinary books, we've delved into the depths of personal development, harnessed the power of intention, and honed the skills essential for entrepreneurial success.

My top five books have served as beacons of wisdom, illuminating the path toward my goals, my dreams, and my highest potential and I hope the same goes for you.

From "The Success Principles" to "The One Thing" each book has offered invaluable insights, actionable strategies, and transformative stories.

But this journey is far from over; it's just the beginning. Armed with the knowledge and inspiration gained from these books, you're now equipped to face the challenges, seize the opportunities, and leave an indelible mark on the world of entrepreneurship that only you can.

Remember, entrepreneurship is a relentless pursuit, a demanding journey that requires unwavering dedication, resilience, belief in oneself and self-growth. It's not a path for the faint-hearted, but it's a path that holds immense rewards for those who dare to tread it.

In the end, your success as an entrepreneur is not solely determined by the businesses you build but by the person you become along the way. As you continue your journey, know that you have the power to create a life that transcends the ordinary, to inspire change, and to leave a lasting legacy.

Thank you for choosing "Revolutionary Reads," for joining me on this journey, and for contributing to the dream of building a library for children in Kenya through the charity Village Impact. Your support means the world. You can see the great work of Village Impact at www.villageimpact.com.

As you close this book and step back into the world of entrepreneurship, remember that you are not alone. You are part of a vibrant community of dreamers, doers, and change-makers. Keep marching to the beat of your own drum, keep pushing boundaries, and keep making a difference.

If you enjoyed this book, I'd be very appreciative if you left a favourable review on Amazon - it's a small gesture with a significant impact.

Here's to your ultimate success, and to the library we dream of building together!

With heartfelt gratitude,

Laurie Joy

23

Resources & Book Links

Wish to order the books discussed? Click below.

Success Principles Jack Canfield: https://amzn.to/3SuJLN2

Your Best Year Ever by Michael Hyatt: https://amzn.to/3Ue6T3s

Atomic Habits by James Clear: https://amzn.to/3Hu9zSZ

How to Build A Storybrand by Donald Miller: https://amzn.to/3SuTRfJ

The One Thing by Gary Keller: https://amzn.to/4ba8VaK

**(full disclosure, I receive a small thank you from Amazon for recommending these books to others).

ChatGPT by OpenAI. (2024, 01, 19). Chapters in Books. [Response to your query]. https://www.openai.com/chatgpt/

About the Author

You can connect with me on:

 https://www.facebook.com/thelauriejoy

Also by Laurie Joy

"Revolutionary Reads II" is your sequel to entrepreneurial enlighten-ment. Discover how to live with intention, embrace your greatness, find inspiration, and create an extraordinary life. Unleash your potential and join the journey of changing the world for the better.

Revolutionary Reads II

The top five books to live with intention, live a life that matters, stop doubting your greatness, have more fun, find inspiration, get extraordinary results & change the world for the better.

www.ingramcontent.com/pod-product-compliance
Lightning Source LLC
Chambersburg PA
CBHW071000290526
45795CB00005B/1716